Captains Blog
START DATE JAN 2011...

...to Boldly Coach where no one has Coached before ...

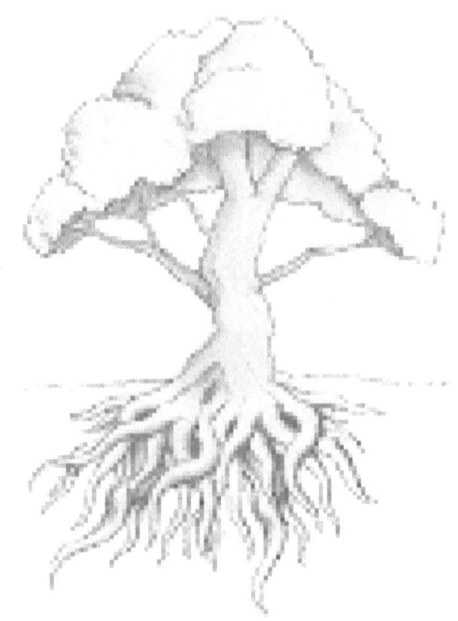

David Holland MBA

© Copyright 2012 David Holland

978-1-291-29088-2
All rights reserved

Contents

INTRODUCTION 5

THE BLOGS 8

It's all about you... 8

Eastern Promise..9

What I learned on a Motorbike in Bali… 10

This is what I did... 12

There are no Ferraris in Metz..................................14

Lessons from the Cosmos... 16

The Ego in the Dark Corner....................................18

How did we get here...? 23

Thinking Outside the Box..27

Capitalism is so over... 30

Are you a Leader or a Manager..?..........................33

Strength in Numbers...36

It's the Recession Stupid..45

R is for Recession...49

Swallows or Hedgehogs..51

Proving a Point... 53

Precessional Effect	55
Life Rules 1.2.3	56
Lights, Camera - ACTION	58
Goals Suck	61
Entrepreneurs Only...	63
W.W.W	66
We are Not Broken	68
Twas the Night before Christmas...	71
Contrary Marketing	73
String Theory	76
ABOUT RESULTS RULES OK	78

Captains Blog
START DATE JAN 2011...

...to Boldly Coach where no one has Coached before ...

Introduction

When I first entered the world of Coaching, Personal Development and Business Growth I quickly learned that there are plenty of labels applied to strategies and tactics that everyone uses naturally – but because there is a label applied to them they have to be relearned and we all have to be Master Wizard Practitioners of some latest craze in order to be able to achieve anything in life.

I started to write my first book sat in this office, sat at this desk exactly two years ago, it is now Friday 7th December 2012, so I thought I had better get this one finished before the predicted end of the world on December 21st - hate leaving things unfinished…

During the last two years I have written another 45 books – this one is number 46 and although a bit of a cheat – it is a compendium of my published Blog posts – I hope you enjoy it and get some ideas you can use, or ideas that will inspire you.

Since I sat here two years ago for the first time, I have learned to enjoy writing and producing content that supports my work as a Coach, Trainer and Speaker. I even have one of my business models being made in to an App for the IPhone; the son of one of my clients is doing it as part of his university degree.

Book 47 to 50 have already been scoped out and will be finished by the end of the year – if the Mayans allow me extra time – and book 51 will be about the Diary of an Entrepreneur co-written with some clients and colleagues, and 52 will be called

Get _ _ _ KED – the art of personal branding and getting ahead in business and life.

So as you can see I have been busy and 2013 looks to be even more exciting. One of the challenges of doing what we do is that we have to not only produce content, ideas and inspiration but live and work by the rules ourselves.

Books have been one of the most transformational aspects of my business, being a published author has opened doors, connected me with like-minded people and enabled me to achieve positive differentiation in what is a very crowded market of Coaches, Consultants and Master Wizards.

So the Captains Blog Start Date January 2011 is the first of a series of books of my scribbling's, thoughts and ideas that if nothing else I hope will give you the confidence to get published yourself and transform you professional life – whatever it is that you do, being published will transform your results.

For 2013, we will continue to boldly coach where no-one has coached before – I am due to return to Nigeria and a visit to Tehran is looking a possibility too.

So enjoy the book, let me know what you think, and I look forward to meeting you at one of our events, or receiving your email.

The Blogs

Friday, 4 March 2011

It's all about you…

Your business, your life and results are all about you…

If you want to get a different output then look at the inputs you are making. Your philosophy towards yourself, your business, team, customers and suppliers will all show up in the results you get.

In business, your profits are just a barometer of how everything else is working. If profits are down, then we have to make an adjustment to your philosophy, or the product, process or promotion activity you are doing, equally if profits are up then this is also a consequence of the quality of activity you are doing.

This is why systems are so important - without systems, all results are a surprise; with systems all results are a consequence of something we can measure, fine tune and adjust.

Results don't just happen - they are always engineered…

Tuesday, 31 May 2011

Eastern Promise...

I was invited to give a series of presentations to business owners and budding entrepreneurs in Bucharest, Romania. After one of the talks, I was approached by someone from the audience and invited to go outside for a cigarette.

I don't smoke, but realised that this was just a code for a discreet chat about the contents of my presentation.

During the discussion, I asked whether he felt that things were better now than they had been under Ceausescu.

His answer surprised me, he said that everyone now had the "freedom to be uncertain", and that whilst he wouldn't want to go back to the days of the dictator, at least back then people had certainty in their lives and things were more predictable.

He explained that getting a car used to mean waiting 5 years just to get a Lada, but at least you got one. Everyone had a job, the state provided everything and life ran according to a comfortable, predictable pattern.

Having had 100% certainty removed from their lives, the people of Romania and other similar Eastern European states, find it challenging to cope with the "freedom to be uncertain" that we take for granted in the "West".

For some, the chalice of freedom has been poisoned with the venom of unpredictability; personal choice and responsibility have replaced comfortable reliance on a Soviet state.

Wednesday, 1 June 2011

What I learned on a Motorbike in Bali...

I rented a small motorbike whilst working in Bali - from memory it was a 175cc Honda.

Leaving Denpasar and following the coast road - Jalan Gumbrih - Lalanglinggah, through Pekutatan I eventually came to a ferry port at the western tip of the Island. Turning right I headed for the hills and the rode through some of the most amazing scenery I have ever seen.

After leaving the main road to head back to the hotel, I noticed that I was being followed by another motorbike and noticed that I had a slight power to weight ratio disadvantage when compared to the young lad following me. On the flat and downhill I could pull away, but uphill he definitely had the advantage...

We "raced" through forest roads until we came to the outskirts of Denpasar and had to stop at a set of traffic lights. While we were stationary he asked me where I was from - so I explained that I was originally from England but that I was living in Las Vegas now. Knowing that I was English, he immediately invited me to go and have tea at his family business.

So I agreed and followed him through some of the poorest housing that I have come across, until we came to what was essentially a shack built out of plywood and corrugated iron. This was the family business - a street cafe serving tea, coffee and snacks.

He insisted that he buy me a cup of tea and a portion of Rojak - spicy fruit salad. He introduced me to his family and was intrigued about this crazy Englishman who lives in Las Vegas and rides a motorbike off the tourist routes.

What I learned was that whilst these people had virtually nothing - they were proud to invite me to eat and drink with them and give me the gift of hospitality and unconditional friendship, I was equally humbled and grateful. To give without the expectation of receiving was my lesson from some of the most genuine people it had become my privilege to know.

Monday, 6 June 2011

This is what I did...

At a recent seminar of mine, one of the audience asked me a question; "If there were two pieces of advice I could give to help someone become more successful, what would they be?"

The question made me think – happens sometimes...

The answer I gave was instinctive, however, with hindsight I think that it was the best answer I could have given. The two pieces of advice that I gave, which have served me well so far in both my personal and professional life, were;

1. **Show Up** – if there is a challenge, meeting, event or opportunity; simply showing up will put you in the top 10% of people. I know that for some of the positions in my early career, I was under qualified and too young – but I showed up when others made excuses about the weather, meetings, and traffic. I have slept in cars and on station platforms to make sure I get to a meeting on time. If you show up you will win – if you don't you can't even participate

2. **Say Yes** – when an opportunity arises, say yes and go for it. I have travelled to 41 Countries, worked in 21 and lived in 3. Saying yes to the sometimes bizarre and unusual requests can lead you on a world tour. I have had plenty of people who have read my story, tell me that they wish

they could have done it – well they could, they just chose not to say yes when it was their time.

There are many more pieces of advice that I could have given including education, training, dedication and commitment – but I was only allowed two, and those were the two I chose.

I was also asked what my goal was when I was 17 – my goal then was to survive until the next morning without being beaten up. I was advised that I needed to have a BFHAG – A Big Fat Hairy Audacious Goal, and that it would inspire me.

Personally I don't want anything Big, Fat and Hairy and Audacious in my life – *sounds like an extra from Wayne's World.* My goals are Big, Athletic, Powerful and Inspiring thanks…

Remember that having a definite fixed Goal can be motivating and inspiring, but it can also be limiting – if my goal had remained to simply survive the night, then I would not have said yes to any opportunity that didn't limit itself to only achieve this.

What have you found works for you - I'm sure there are many different strategies that have worked, and I'd like to hear about them...

Tuesday, 26 July 2011

There are no Ferraris in Metz...

August is a strange time in France - everyone goes on holiday for the month…

I took my car into the local garage for repairs on Tuesday, only to be warned that if they couldn't fix it by Friday - *it would be September before I got it back...*

As it is most businesses don't open up until 10.00 am on a Monday, on Sunday everything is closed and they still find time for a two hour lunch break from 12.00 until 2.00pm...

We moved here about 18 months ago from Las Vegas in the USA - which is about as far as you can get culturally from rural France. In Vegas, everything is open 24 Hrs. a day, the casinos never close, and just about anything can be driven through or delivered to your home or hotel room.

So what..?

In Las Vegas we lived in a gated community with cameras, security guards and high walls to protect us, guns were in easy circulation and a search on the web revealed just how many convicted criminals lived in close proximity. Vegas is a transient city with great spirit but no heart; it is the American Dream on megawatt life support where alcohol fuelled highs are more than matched by acidic black jack and roulette induced desperation. Note - *the casinos **always** win in the end...*

The French do things differently, there are no guns, no cameras, and drugs are what you take when you have a headache. There is a value put on family community and quality of life - no one cares what car you drive, there are no Ferraris in Metz. What counts is lifestyle, choosing to take lunch, taking the month off, spending time with family and friends - no one actually needs 24hr shopping; I still can't remember who voted for that in the first place. Miraculously, we somehow manage to survive with the shops only open 6 days a week...

So what are you living the Vegas life or the Metz life - are you letting the glamour and the glitz dazzle your path to happiness, are you working 90 hours a week because you think it's how it has to be, are you substituting your real life with a fragile synthetic veneer of material acquisitions?

Metaphorically, everyone should holiday in Las Vegas and experience the energy, passion, fun and the endless possibilities. However, everyone should remember that in reality they need to live in France...

I wonder if that is where all the French go in August...?

Saturday, 30 July 2011

Lessons from the Cosmos...

It was a very clear night last night - *and it had stayed warm too...*

There is something serene about star gazing, I don't know all the constellations and I can't find Venus or Mars, but sitting there with a glass of Southern Comfort on the rocks and contemplating the biggest questions we have, was magical...

As my eyes became accustomed to the dark, more stars appeared, and if I used my peripheral vision rather than looking directly at them I started to see clusters and detail that were not there before.

After a few minutes I spotted a plane - it was moving and flashing lights - so even I knew it wasn't Mars. Then in the corner of my eye I spotted a feint dot of light moving across the sky - no flashing lights.

It was a satellite - and as it passed overhead, I was reminded of the lyrics to a song by Billy Bragg - New England, part of which goes like this...

"I saw two shooting stars last night, I wished on them but they were only satellites, it's wrong to wish on space hardware..."

As the words came into my head, I thought to myself how cool it would be if after having seen the satellite, I now saw two shooting stars to complete the event...

Then - within seconds a bright "shooting star" raced across the sky, and within two minutes another even brighter than the first. I had seen the shooting stars that I had imagined, the picture was complete, and I had Goosebumps...

So what lessons did I learn from this...

1. To find what you are looking for you have to know where to look and when is the best time. We have to be present in our own lives and in the situations that will move us forwards - in the case of shooting stars; looking up, at night is a good start...

2. In life and business, we need patience, we need to become accustomed to our environment and put ourselves in situations that allow opportunities to become manifest to us. It takes time, if we rush and chase too hard; we will miss the very things we desire.

3. Sometimes our results come from the periphery - we need focus but we also need to watch the edges, because that's where the best ideas and opportunities may come from - the Law of Precession...

4. When we have a vision or an idea, when we are clear about what we want, we will recognise the opportunities and events that accord with us. Without a vision, life is a random set of events, with vision and dreams, the same events have purpose and significance.

Monday, 8 August 2011

The Ego in the Dark Corner...

Sometimes, does it all just feel like your business isn't working?

Your clients are a pain in the neck, cash flow is tight, you're working harder than you team, and your marketing sucks, you are grumpy with your partner, the kids hide from you and even the dog keeps out of your way...

Sound familiar? - There are two facts about this situation;

1. **It is only true to you** - you just paint a dark picture because it fits in your dark corner at the moment...

2. **You are not alone** - welcome to being in business. Guess what, everyone goes through this at some time...

So what to do...

First, remember that your view of the world is just that - your view. You make your view true for you by finding evidence and "facts" to support your belief that everything is going against you. You may even find that if you look really hard you can find other people who have a similar picture of the world - so then you can confirm your beliefs with negative affirmations and third party validations too - bravo, that should help..

Your physiology follows your emotional state - if you are unhappy, frustrated or angry, it will show. This will affect your behaviour, your work and your relationships. If you believe things are bad then you will create the environment for those "bad things" to become manifest to you.

Beliefs + (Thoughts x Actions) = Results

If you start the equation with a negative Belief – regardless of how positive your Thoughts and Actions are – the resultant Result will always be negative...

Imagine that we rate your Beliefs, Thoughts and Actions on a scale of -10 to +10 with -10 being very low or negative and +10 being very high and positive.

Let's say that your results look like this;

Beliefs = -7, Thoughts = +2, Actions = +8

This means that whilst your beliefs are negative, you're Thoughts, (hoping and praying) that things will get better, are +2 and your Actions are + 9 – *you are really busy...*

This is what your Result will be...

-7 + (2 x 8) = **-23**

It all starts with a belief...

If you decide to believe that, for example, social media, telemarketing or networking (pick anything from training to coaching, customer service to budgeting) won't work in your business - then guess what; it won't because you will sabotage the process and find reasons to justify why in your "special business" these strategies don't work - *then you will look for facts to back up your argument.*

If you search on Google for "social media doesn't work" you will get 406 Million results - now you can even write a book on how you always knew that social media wouldn't work - your ego will be inflated and you will be vindicated because you were right..

If however you search on Google for "social media does work" you will get 747 Million results - but because these facts are uncomfortable to your ego, you decide to ignore this and revert back to your comfortable dark corner safe with your other evidence. Doh..!

This is painful because it means that you will have to concede that you are not the master of the entire universe and that, in fact, the laws of physics do apply to you.

So Rule 1 - drop the ego and choose a different belief.

Whatever Belief you choose, will manifest itself in your business and in your life – you will make it happen and attract the circumstances to yourself that will satisfy your ego's demands for vindication.

One of the best ways to change a belief is knowledge and education – read books, watch videos, listen to stories of those who you actually want to be like. It isn't that you will copy what they did, or have to do what they did – it is just that when you are open to the possibility of a different outcome, your belief changes and therefore so will your Thoughts, Actions and Reactions.

Using the formula above; let's just assume that your Belief shifts to +2, this is what happens;

$2 + (2 \times 8) = \mathbf{18}$

A positive result – in fact for a 9 point movement in Beliefs, you have achieved a 41 point shift in your Results...

Rule 2 – it's OK to get help...

This is another huge challenge to the ego – especially us guys. We are the hunter killers, we bring meat and make fire, and we are the stealthy predators. Without help and support, we build our business and our income simply because we are the alpha male – *and we never cry either...*

How is that working for you...?

What would you rather have, a huge balance sheet or a huge ego..?

The two are generally mutually exclusive, one is very attractive, and the other isn't.

Man or woman – it doesn't matter, reaching out and asking someone to help you is a great step in changing your beliefs; Coaching works not because the Coach knows all the answers, rather they ask the right questions to challenge your Beliefs and adapt your Thoughts and Actions.

If you have got this far, then we should talk – providing of course your ego doesn't stop you pressing send on the email…

Remember, the easiest way to get out of your dark corner is to turn the light on – *it just maybe that someone else needs to show you where the switch is…*

Friday, 19 August 2011

How did we get here...?

I write either late at night or early in the morning - I prefer mornings as there is something reassuring about the sunrise that confirms my belief in immortality...

So here I sit at 03.30, mug of tea in hand – and a blank screen in front of me. I have been invited to write a compelling chapter for a new book on the subject of Business Accounts...

So you won't be surprised to know that I have "writers block" – and in order to remove the block I have started playing on the internet.

At first I did an ego search – typed my own name into Google – but that drummer out of Judas Priest still pops up along with the Jazz Musician of the same name. No fun there...

It is now 03.40 so I have decided to type in "conspiracy theories" just for the heck of it...

So far I have learned that man didn't land on the Moon, 9/11 was planned by the CIA, Elvis is actually alive and the Philadelphia experiment really happened – *they are all on the internet so they must be true*...!

Something has just caught my eye – and it has to do with the Banking System...

Now, I do know that I need to tread carefully here, and that there are plenty of cranks and nut cases out there who are probably uploading bizarre facts and theories dreamt up in an alcohol induced haze – but there is something here that is just plain interesting, and whether it is true or not doesn't matter; it just seems to make sense...

How did we arrive in this financial mess, where the USA has a "debt clock" located in Times Square. The Clock was first installed by Seymour Durst on Feb 20th 1989 in order to raise awareness of the consequences of the economic policies of the Reagan era.

Back in 1989 – just 22 years ago – the USA had a debt of $2.7 Trillion. Then in late September 2008 the clock ran out of digits – the debt in the USA passed $10 Trillion and the digital "clock" needed an extra digit to display the amount.

Checking the value of the USA Debt today at 04.00 – it stands at around $14.5 Trillion. So that means that in the last 22 years the amount of US debt has increased by a total of $11.8 Trillion, which looks like this $11,800,000,000,000. My calculator won't accept numbers that big so I have now switched to Excel to calculate that on average, every day , the USA has been getting deeper into debt to the tune of **$1.5 Billion** every Day or $62,500,00 every hour, about $1,000,000 every minute..

Looks like there is something wrong...

So how did we get here…?

Look back in time to the control of the Money Supply to find out how we arrived at this ridiculous situation. Look at the rise of Fractional Reserve banking and the current banking system, check out what happened to the tally stick system in the UK, and look at the how the Federal Reserve – which is a privately owned corporation – controls the economy of the USA and effectively those of Europe too…

My point is this – it is not the things that we can predict that will have the greatest effect upon us, whether positive or negative. It is always the unseen actions that we can't see coming that have the most dramatic effect – and those dramatic effects are the manifestations of actions and decisions that have already taken place, so you can't change them.

The financial crisis we are currently experiencing is the consequence of bright men in dark suits making huge amounts of money at the expense of the other 99.9% of the population – remember money does not disappear; it simply transfers to someone else…

So plan for what you know, but always prepare for the unexpected – for that is where success and failure are found. Be grateful for your wins and chastened by your losses, but remember always that they both may simply be symptoms of someone else's turn of the card…

Above all – enjoy the ride, make it fun, play nice and look after what no one can take away from you; your spirit, your relationships and your humanity. Travel, do crazy stuff like the world ends tomorrow – nothing you can do will be as stupid as the men in dark suits who have got it wrong by $1m every minute...

Oh, and recycle your plastic too.

At least now I have a chapter to write of the book – and it is now 04.45, here in the Moselle...

Monday, 22 August 2011

Thinking Outside the Box...

I found this article whilst surfing the Web - I don't know who originated it so I can't give appropriate credit for it. If I find out, then of course I will...

Some time ago a lecturer received a call from a colleague. He was about to give a student a zero for his answer to a physics question, while the student claimed a perfect score. The instructor and the student agreed to an impartial arbiter, and he was selected.

The Examination Question read as follows;

SHOW HOW IS IT POSSIBLE TO DETERMINE THE HEIGHT OF A TALL BUILDING WITH THE AID OF A BAROMETER

The student had answered, "Take the barometer to the top of the building, attach a long rope to it, lower it to the street, and then bring the rope up, measuring the length of the rope. The length of the rope is the height of the building."

The student really had a strong case for full credit since he had really answered the question completely and correctly! On the other hand, if full credit were given, it could well contribute to a high grade in his physics course and to certify competence in physics, but the answer did not confirm this.

The lecturer then suggested that the student have another try. The student was given six minutes to answer the question with the warning that the answer should show some knowledge of physics. At the end of five minutes, he had not written anything. He was asked if he wished to give up, but he said he had many answers to this problem; he was just thinking of the best one. The lecturer excused himself for interrupting him and asked him to please go on.

In the next minute, he dashed off his answer which read: "Take the barometer to the top of the building and lean over the edge of the roof. Drop the barometer, timing its fall with a stopwatch. Then, using the formula X= 0.5 (A T2) calculate the height of the building."

At this point, the lecturer asked the original instructor if he would give up. He conceded, and gave the student almost full credit. While leaving his colleague's office, the lecturer recalled that the student had said that he had other answers to the problem, so he asked him what they were.

"Well," said the student, "there are many ways of getting the height of a tall building with the aid of a barometer. For example, you could take the barometer out on a sunny day and measure the height of the barometer, the length of its shadow, and the length of the shadow of the building, and by the use of simple proportion, determine the height of the building."

"Fine," the lecturer said, "and others?"

"Yes," said the student, "there is a very basic measurement method you will like. In this method, you take the barometer and begin to walk up the stairs. As you climb the stairs, you mark off the length of the barometer along the wall. You then count the number of marks, and this will give you the height of the building in barometer units."

"A very direct method."

"Of course, if you want a more sophisticated method, you can tie the barometer to the end of a string, swing it as a pendulum, and determine the value of g at the street level and at the top of the building. From the difference between the two values of g, the height of the building, in principle, can be calculated."

"On this same tact, you could take the barometer to the top of the building, attach a long rope to it, lower it to just above the street, and then swing it as a pendulum. You could then calculate the height of the building by the period of the precession".

"Finally," he concluded, "there are many other ways of solving the problem.

Probably the best," he said, "is to take the barometer to the basement and knock on the superintendent's door. When the superintendent answers, you speak to him as follows: 'Mr. Superintendent, here is a fine barometer. If you will tell me the height of the building, I will give you this barometer."

At this point, the student was asked if he really did not know the conventional answer to this question. He admitted that he did, but said that he was fed up with high school and college instructors trying to teach him how to think.

The student was Neils Bohr and the arbiter was Ernest Rutherford.

Tuesday, 4 October 2011

Capitalism is so over...

Capitalism isn't working...

The Banks and Financial institutions have led us all to the current situation. A mixture of Fractional Reserve Banking, Interest on Loans and greed for future profits out of complex financial instruments have destroyed the "system" that we thought would help and support us in life and in business.

We seem to have forgotten that, as business owner entrepreneurs, we have to add value to something before we sell it – parasitically investing in the stock market, a property portfolio, or even a MLM scheme – doesn't add value to anyone. The only reason that these activities produce a "profit" is because of the way the current system is flawed through its dependency on money creation and inflationary growth that fuels the ever increasing debt stream.

So what is the way forwards for business owners like us – we can blame the banks, take to the streets and bemoan the systematic profiteering of the 1% of the world population that own 40% of its assets – or we can step up and actually change the way we operate, stop playing their game and start to take back credible control.

Here's how we do it.

First, get your business and your life debt free – as business owners this is a primary objective. Making profit just to pay interest to the bank on money they created out of nothing in the first place is a waste of your efforts.

Grow your business with "no money down" – give great customer service, add real value, innovate and put the passion back into your team to deliver a remarkable experience and you will generate profits and cash to clear the loans.

Second, recognise that your pension, stock portfolio and options are all synthetic and will have no value in the future. Your business is your future, you legacy and your long term income stream. Build your business as if you will keep it for life – you may not have to work there all the time – but it will sustain you, your family and those who work for you much more effectively than some pension or investment fund that produces more bonuses for the bankers than future pensions for you.

Third, remember that greed is not good – we are here to make a profit and build a lifestyle. The days when we can do this at the expense of others and cause massive inequality of income and resources are over – remember someone has to actually work hard at some point in the system, and we have a collective responsibility to contribute as well as extract value from it.

Employ people and pay them well for working hard for you – give them stability and brightness of future – not everyone wants the "excitement" of business ownership.

We are the 99% - we can make the changes – look at what is happening in the USA – we have a golden opportunity to make a capital based economy that works; not just for the pinstriped bankers and investors but everyone. The 99% didn't cause the chaos, but with a change of approach we can correct it…

Wednesday, 2 November 2011

Are you a Leader or a Manager..?

No one truly understands Leadership – that is why so many books are written about it, with each author giving their own "formula" for success. I have read dozens of them and although the titles often include the term "Leadership" – what they are essentially talking about is how to get other people to do something they wouldn't otherwise do in exchange for money or reward.

This is not **Leadership** – this is **Management**.

I have seen plenty of "Leaders" who hide behind the veil of Management in the belief that their position within a corporate structure somehow transforms them into gurus and experts that should be listened to and copied at every opportunity. Take away their position in the company and they crumble, very few will actually admit that they became good Managers and anointed Leaders simply because of the elevated positions they were promoted to in someone else's organisation; they believe it was them all along…

It is relatively easy to be a great leader when you pay salaries to everyone so that they follow you, and if they don't follow you; they get fired…

So what is Leadership..?

First, Managers do not need to be Leaders – they have authority given to them; they have rules, regulations and procedures to use to control people in order to produce a specific result. If a Manager is a Leader as well – then they will be truly effective and it will show in their results and in the spirit and culture of their company.

Second, Leaders do not need to be good Managers – they lead by example with the consent of their teams and those associated with their cause or vision. Leaders don't pay people to follow them; they attract and inspire them to.

In business we have to be Leaders in our own respective fields, whether that is thought, technology, service, product or quality. Our clients have a choice, and only those who are capable of leading and inspiring their teams and their clients will be truly successful. A great Leader will hire great Managers and attract people, clients and associates to achieve the Vision.

So a question for you – who is following you without being paid to do so…?

How would you have to behave, what value would you need to add and how inspiring and attractive would you need to become such that you were truly a Leader in your field..?

Leadership is about Vision, Passion and Commitment to a cause or objective – this will encourage people to follow you or decide not to – most leaders are loved and despised equally; mediocrity is not an effective Leadership position.

To be a great Leader become evangelical about whom you really are, what you do, why you do it and your purpose in life – it's time to stand for something and go public. Then take action to achieve your visions and dreams; the right people will follow you and the Leader will emerge.

Remember, Managers get Qualified

–

Leaders get Identified

Monday, 30 January 2012

Strength in Numbers...

A Brand is one of the most valuable, intangible and indefinite assets that a company can have. Organisations such as McDonalds, Coca Cola, Nike, Google, and Virgin have spent millions building up their reputation and branding through images, logo's and strap lines.

Having a brand removes the uncertainty from the buying process – the more certainty surrounding a purchase the less the resistance will be to making it. Conversely, the more uncertainty surrounding a buying decision, the higher the levels of resistance that will have to be overcome in order for the purchase to be completed.

Branding makes the invisible more visible; the intangible more tangible and the uncertain more certain. All a brand essentially does is allow us to make emotional or instinctive decisions based on perceptions of quality, value and service represented by the Brand such that we don't need to logically justify the emotional decisions we make. IBM famously used the advertising slogan – "no one gets fired for buying IBM..."

If in doubt and in the absence of other information we will tend to be attracted to a recognised brand rather than take the "risk" buying something that is unknown to us and or potentially of lower quality, reliability or levels of consistency. I have used the example of McDonalds for demonstration purposes in the image, but the same concept can be applied to Hilton, The Wynn Las Vegas, Gucci or BMW.

The higher the levels of Brand Recognition; the lower the resistance to purchase.

Rule # 1 – consistent, predictable and branded mediocrity will beat occasional uncertain excellence.

In the absence of a recognised brand, buyers will tend to be more cautious – looking for evidence to support their buying process. In the medium size business sector we are not in the business of building a brand – we are in the business of building reputation and it is the transmission and perception of our reputation that attracts prospective clients to us whilst the consistent delivery of experiences that exceed expectations, keeps customers returning to us on a regular basis.

Remember that we have to replace the power of a brand; we are selling what is essentially an invisible, intangible service (at least until it is experienced for the first time...) and we have a number of strategies available that will enable us to achieve this.

Rule # 2 – in the absence of a Brand – other evidence is needed in order to make a buying decision.

In his book "Influence" Dr Robert Cialdini explains the Psychology of getting customers to say "yes" and proposes six keys of influence that conspire either with us or against us when we are marketing and presenting information about our services – this is where we can win when we come up against bigger or more easily recognised brands.

a. **Reciprocation**

   i. **Explanation** – we are obliged to respond to the experiences we have. If I buy you a drink at the bar, you have a natural obligation to return the favour. This works in the positive and the negative, remember an eye for an eye and a tooth for a tooth.

   ii. **Application** – people will spread the word about the experiences they have when they buy from us. A mediocre experience may not generate any feedback at all and a bad experience is likely to trigger a negative response of some sort, however, it usually takes an amazing experience to elicit a positive comment. It is the generation of these positive responses that must be our objective. We need to exceed the expectations of our clients, such that not only the service they receive, but the context in which it is provided, triggers a positive reciprocation of testimonials, referrals and reputation development.

b. **Consistency**

   i. **Explanation** – people generally don't want high levels of uncertainty or perceived risk when it comes to making a buying decision. They will look for signs of consistency and trust such that they have the belief that we not only deliver on our promises, but deliver on them consistently and predictably every time.

ii. **Application** – having systems in place that ensure excellence is the surest way of achieving this. There are numerous ways that organisations have achieved this from the well-known Franchise organisations to Zappos, Cirque Du Soleil, Ritz Carlton Group, Apple and Nordstroms.

c. **Social Proof**

   i. **Explanation** - people will look to other independent people for opinions about our services. People like to have certainty when making any decision and a contributory factor to developing this certainty is what other people say about us.

   ii. **Application** – testimonials and customer feedback is critical here, as is "collective evidence" or the power associated with being part of an organisation or group. If as the business owner you say something positive about your venue; it's sales and marketing. If a client says something positive about your venue; it's the truth – in the eyes of your prospects. Social Proof is how we can enable our prospects not only to emotionally engage with our business, making the invisible visible and the intangible tangible; but it limits the need for logic i.e. price comparisons and discount discussions to enter into the process.

Rule # 3 – People do not buy on price – *unless we let them.*

d. Authority

i. **Explanation** – we automatically trust those who either are or appear to be experts in their field. If someone who looks like a dentist prepares you for root canal treatment you believe that they know what they are doing; have you ever asked to see the qualifications or certificates that your Doctor or Dentist have..?

ii. **Application** – this is the first instance where the power of the group comes into force. Being associated with a recognised group or collective, automatically suggests that you have "qualified" to be included and are therefore better, of higher quality and standards than those who do not qualify to be part of the group. Maintaining high standards and having specific objectives towards excellence, that can be measured, will enable the power and perception of authority suggested by inclusion within the group or association to be kept high – membership is a privilege.

e. Liking

i. **Explanation** – we tend to buy from people we like and are like. The same goes for organisations, we will buy from them when they resonate with us and we like, not just the people within them but the Philosophy and Values that an organisation demonstrates.

ii. **Application** – being public with the Philosophy and Values of your organisation, letting people connect with your team with images and even video is a great way to build rapport with your clients even before they have bought. It is the degree of liking that will also determine the extent to which they come back and buy from you in the future. Training and passionate evangelical commitment to excellence, standards and the entire customer experience are key here.

f. Scarcity

i. **Explanation** – simply put we want what we can't have, and attribute higher value to that which is scarce or appears to be scarce.

ii. **Application** – this again is where exclusivity and the power and perceived value of the group can be used to our advantage. It is unlikely that any of us can actually define what our market share or market penetration is in terms of the total UK market, and if we can our shares will be so low that they are almost meaningless. Let's say you have 1% of the total Market for Venues and Conference events in the UK – you cannot possibly cope with all of it so by definition you are a niche player, customers are abundant and you are the scarce resource – providing of course you standards and performance are exceptional.

Being part of an exclusive group means that the standards and reputation that the group stands for are only available through members of that group

– that in itself is highly attractive and establishes scarcity simply through membership and association with the group

Rule # 4 – A Quality Niche business must beat their more recognised branded competitors in terms of quality, service, uniqueness and consistency; gather together in groups and shout loud so that they don't have to also beat them on price.

The Ultimate Question

Accepting that we need to overcome any potential resistance in the absence of strong branding – we clearly need to achieve our competitive advantage through service and quality differentiation and not price.

Holding ourselves accountable to the highest standards and measuring our performance against them whilst challenging is in reality the only option we have either individually or even more powerfully; as part of a powerful, strong and recognised collective or group.

Traditionally, customer feedback was based on subjective matters, scored over a range of 1 to 5 or based on comments and "feedback" even nominating individuals for praise. In reality and to truly get an objective measure of performance, accepting that clients buy emotionally, we need to assess their levels of emotional engagement with the service that we provide. Emotional purchases need emotional measures not logical ones; otherwise there is incongruence in the process.

In the book "The Ultimate Question" Fred Riechheld defines a revolutionary system of engaging clients in an emotionally driven response process that simply requires them to answer a simple question.

"On a scale of 0 to 10 where 0 means "not at all likely" and 10 means "extremely likely" how likely is it that you would recommend XXXXXXX to a friend or colleague.

Whilst this sounds very simple it is the scoring method that forces us to raise the bar of quality, service and uniqueness. Under traditional conditions, when asking survey questions involving a scale of 1 to 10 we would have been satisfied with an average score of say 80% - on the face of it this looks good.

The Net Promoter Score is different, the scoring is heavily weighted such that it represents a very harsh and what may at first sight appear to be somewhat unfair.

The scoring system works like this;

0 1 2 3 4 5 6 7 8 9 10

Scoring between 0 and 6 results in a score of -1

Scoring a 7 or 8 results in a score of 0

Scoring a 9 or 10 results in a score of +1

What this means that is in order to score a maximum 100 from 100 questions the scores have to be either 9 or 10; as soon as the scores start to drop to 8 or 7 or even lower the scores drop dramatically – if everyone scored our business at 8 out 10, instead of being happy and satisfied with 80% under the traditional methods of rating performance, under the Net Promoter Scoring system – *we achieve a score of 0*

What this means that is that in order to achieve high scores under these conditions we need to be truly excellent and deliver remarkable service on a consistent basis – this is a tough rule and holds us accountable to the highest of standards.

See Rule # 4 for the reason this is so important...

The benefits of this process are amplified when there is a group or association of companies that combine and compare scores under this system. Being part of the group allows best practice to be shared, standards and performance to be monitored, with collective targets for improvement being agreed between the members – the collective strength of the group is stronger than the strength of an individual.

Tuesday, 7 February 2012

It's the Recession Stupid...

One of the most frequent questions I get asked by business people, whether it is when I'm on stage, with a client or at an event is – "how can we grow in a recession..?"

Even when I reached out to my network and asked for ideas for a title of a new event, EBook or workshop – the instant response was the same – "how can we grow in a recession..?"

So this Blog is a prelude to an EBook, a Workshop and a Business Master Class event that will seek to answer this very question. If you'd like more details on these events, see the contact information on our website – or simply email me on davidholland@resultsrulesok.com

First, there are two harsh realities of business, the people that manage them and the environment in which they operate – I will explain both realities by telling a couple stories that I hope will bring clarity...

Harsh Reality # 1 – It's not about the Recession it's all about You.

When the market is buoyant, cash is available, companies are expanding and recruiting, confidence is up and life is good – businesses do well. In fact under those conditions, just about any business will do well regardless of how it is built, run and managed. All boats rise on the incoming tide...

When business is good there is a tendency (*and I know this won't apply to you*) for some other business people to associate the business success with them; it's their ideas, direction, inspiration and business intellect.

When business dips and the results stagnate or decline, it is these same other business people who blame the market (recession is such a convenient term), the Banks, the Government, Customers, Employees – in fact anything is blamed rather than the unfortunate Harsh Reality that they simply do not know what they are doing. More to the point, they never did – they were successful in spite of themselves, the historic strength of the market simply masked over the cracks in their ability and lulled them into a false sense of security; their self-belief and ego being massaged by the returns on the balance sheet.

So the first Harsh Reality is to recognise, or of course for others to recognise, that the Recession is just an excuse and that the results in any business are a direct reflection of the ability, knowledge, passion and skills of the people who run it – if you want better results, get better ability, knowledge, passion and skills.

The challenge here is that this is a potentially huge slap in the face to the ego of these other business people. Admitting that we need more knowledge and passion suggest that we are not as clever or grand as we thought we were and have to adapt our identity from being the "know it all guru.." to become the eager student...

Harsh Reality # 2 – It's not about the Recession and it's not about anyone else.

In the USA a business owner who happened to be a reasonably recent immigrant there was being interviewed about the success he had achieved in developing a chain of Coffee shops in a large east coast city. From humble beginnings, in spite of English not being his first language, and with little money he had built a successful and thriving business that was the envy of others in the sector.

The interviewer introduced him onto the radio show and the first question was.

"so tell us, how you built this thriving business in the middle of the deepest recession since the 1930's..?"

His answer was perfect and in my view should be printed on not only the mind but the business cards and store fronts of every business owner.

"I didn't know there was a recession, no one told me…"

This simple story explains exactly why some people have struggling businesses – they are told that things are tough, they focus on it and guess what; things get tough…

Harsh Reality #2 is that you absolutely must keep focussed on your business, not listening to the news, reading the headlines, or having pity parties with the poor souls who read the Daily Mail, Express, Mirror etc. There is only one page in a newspaper that is factual – and it is at the back, it reports the actual scores recorded in the football.

It could also be argued that the statistics on page 3 of **The Sun** are accurate but that is a different discussion…

Remove from your network all negativity, speculation and hearsay – this may involve not talking to certain people – *and you know who they are; yes you do..!*

Put into your network bright intelligent enthusiastic people who believe in you, will help support and guide you. Build clarity of your vision, focus on you customer and the experience they have when the trade with you – focus on simply being the best there is and then it doesn't matter what the market is doing, you will be doing great…

Sometimes ignorance is indeed bliss…

Sunday, 26 February 2012

R is for Recession…

It is unfortunate that when business is good we believe that it is due to our knowledge, passion and entrepreneurial skills, however, when business is not so good we blame the recession, the government or our customers. On an incoming tide, all boats rise and so it is with companies in a strong market; whatever we do will probably work, and sometimes a business can be successful *in spite* of the owners knowledge passion and skills…

When business is tough we realise that what we used to do simply doesn't work, the tide is flowing against us and we have to find "new" ways of attracting customers and growing our sales. In reality we don't need to find any "new" ways at all – we just need to go back the basic principles that the levels of our previous success had afforded us the luxury of ignoring.

R is for Results – *there are* **5 Principles** *to follow to get Results…*

1. **Philosophy** – be clear on your goals, standards and values. Your business will be a reflection of you and it may be that you need to change, learn new skills or think differently.

2. **Product** – is your product or service truly excellent? Is what you do attractive and valuable to your clients, is it unique and different from your competition?

3. **Process** – does your business only run when you are there? Remember, it is not what you supply but the context in which you supply it that makes the difference – is excellence systemised, or is it a lucky random occurrence?

4. **Promotion** – are you marketing your business effectively? Are you sending compelling messages to your defined target market and can you measure the results you are achieving?

5. **Profit** – is not your objective. Profit is a symptom of everything else that happens in your business, the outcome of the first 4 Principles. If your profit is not where you need it to be, simply look at your Philosophy, Product, Process or Promotion to find the solution.

The **5 Principles** should be approached in sequence – it is no good having great Promotional activity if your Product and Process is not up to scratch for example. In my experience, we must start with ourselves – challenge ourselves to learn adapt and change at the same pace as the environment changes around us; only then will everything else fall into place.

Monday, 27 February 2012

Swallows or Hedgehogs...

Hedgehogs are one of only three UK mammals that have the ability to hibernate. They will hibernate through the winter depending upon the availability of food. When times are tough they roll into a ball and hibernate – waiting until things improve and their food supply becomes available again before they wake up.

Hedgehogs will even change their diets according to what is available and frequently eat foods that are high in fat and sugar although their metabolism is designed for low fat protein rich foods. This leads to cases of fatty liver and heart disease being quite common.

British Swallows spend their winter in South Africa, covering up to 200 miles a day at speeds of up to 35mph. Swallows value consistency and understand that in order to achieve it they have to go somewhere different in order to achieve it. The journey is hazardous and sometimes they will die of exhaustion as they fly over the Sahara, but they value consistent temperatures and food supply above the hardship of making the actual journey.

In business and life we have a choice – we can be either a Hedgehog or a Swallow.

The Hedgehog business is cyclical; the results look like a roller coaster, when times are good life is good, when times are tough a Hedgehog business will roll into a ball and defend itself, and if sales dry up it will go into hibernation – we call it denial or insolvency.

The Swallow business endures the same cycles as the Hedgehog but the response is different. The Swallow takes the risk of changing its environment, leaving what is comfortable and embarking on a journey that whilst dangerous, has the potential to deliver abundance and security; and most of all, continuity...

So what type of business does the best – when the markets are good, business will be good and staying put and reaping the benefits of an abundant harvest looks like a sensible and easy option. When winter arrives in the form of a recession, staying put is not an option, and success will be achieved only by taking the risk of doing something different; metaphorically flying over the Sahara.

The business environment has changed, it is not that is any harder than it was before, it is just that we need to change what we do and where we go in order to achieve the same levels of success. The Hedgehog mentality of hibernation in the hope that things will get better doesn't work, the recession will last longer than you reserves of cash.

Swallows will win the day. They always did, just that Hedgehogs justified their behaviour when times were good because it seemed to work for them. Looking for new markets, innovations and customers, taking the risk of the new and daring to take the journey is where the Swallows business attitude will win.

Plus, if I am going to fall over - I would much rather do it soaring over the African Plains than hiding under a hedge in West Bromwich. It's a choice...

Monday, 26 March 2012

Proving a Point...

I remember being told that I had two choices in Careers at school - either to go down the Pit or join the Infantry...

I also remember running away to London to create my own future at the age of 17 - I was asked if I did it to prove "them" wrong. I knew that "they" were wrong already; I didn't need to prove that, they had demonstrated that through their words and actions.

What I did have to do was prove myself right - I developed an "inner" belief in myself that shielded me from the negative views of others, that has stayed with me to this day.

At 17 however, I ended up sleeping on platforms and carriages courtesy of British Rail, or eating at the Charity Shelters courtesy of the Red Cross - but I always believed, and Lynn believed in me too - if you believe strong enough then reality catches up eventually...

Of course, the belief may have been overstated at the time - but the more trust I have had in myself the more I have been able to prove myself right. This has enabled me to stay married for 26 years so far - in spite of what the family had to say - live in three countries, get my MBA and write 36 books...

It's not what other people think about you that is important, it is what you think about yourself that matters. If I had listened to the external voices back then, I would have been in a very different place now.

The top three life lessons that I have learned so far, that I hope will help you on your journey;

1. Trust your instinct...

2. Love unconditionally...

3. Say Yes...

Wednesday, 2 May 2012

Precessional Effect

Around 12 months ago I published my first book - **Life RULES OK**. A semi biographical story of personal growth, development and success - with some of the lessons I have learned so far on my journey to date.

For those of you that have published a book, you will know what it feels like to hold a finished piece of work in your hands, and the sense of pride that having completed the work brings. I wrote the book with the intention of inspiring people - or just one person maybe - to avoid some of the "excitement" I had experienced in my teens.

So keen was I to get the message out that we ran seminars and workshops where I gave books away to anyone who would turn up to an event - just to get the message out. Turns out that this was perhaps a mistake…

About two weeks ago I received an Email from a young lady who had bought my book from a local charity shop - (someone I gave the book to had chosen to pass it on..) and she was so moved by the content that she was compelled to summarise the material in the form of a Poem;

Life Rules 1.2.3

This is the way I clearly see
As we move away
We leave behind
What keeps us stuck?
As life was struck

To change our views
To match values
To keep open minded
As visions were blinded
To move forward

To embrace the fear
To keep hold of our dreams
Of ones we see dear
Life rules 1.2.3
This is the way
I clearly see
As my pictures
Profoundly become me

Emma Islip - 2012

Now the lesson here for me is that giving something away does not in itself generate any benefit, however the precessional effect - if the book had not been donated to the Charity Shop - can be amazing...

The Universe acts in mysterious ways - I got the effect I wanted but not in the method I anticipated. This happens in Life and in Business so often...

If you want to give your God a good laugh - tell her your plans for the future...

Wednesday, 9 May 2012

Lights, Camera - ACTION

I never really understood how to formulate a "Goal" – seemed to be difficult for me to choose just one "thing" or result…

Instead I found that by simply imagining "how cool would it be if…" I could create a future scene that included a variety of things..

For example, I used to think it "would be really cool" to actually live and work in the USA – I could visualise the cars, the buildings, and the people I could meet. I had a movie in my mind of what life could be like, how people would react to my accent, the air temperature and how I would be able to ride a Harley Davidson to Death Valley, or drive a ridiculous SUV over the Hoover Dam…

It wasn't a Goal, it was more than that, it was a ready-made show reel in which I was the Director, Producer, Writer and Star – to me it was it was real, I could play the movie to myself in my mind whenever I wished…

That was when I was 17 – at that time life was not so sparkly and bright – eating cold food in a damp flat, or sleeping on the Central Line to keep warm was a million miles away from the USA…

Now let's scroll forwards – on the 31st March 2008 I receive a telephone call. Would I like to take my self my business and my family to live and work in the USA – Las Vegas to be precise…?

My instant response was yes – within 2 weeks I was there, we sold everything and moved to the USA, we had a fabulous time there for two years. I bought the Harley Davidson and the SUV rode to Death Valley and drove over the Hoover Dam.

Note that this actually took 25 years to achieve - and to go from Ponders End to Las Vegas took plenty of work, learning, winning, losing, blood sweat and tears...

After a while we started to realise that actually, France was more in tune with our personal and professional ambitions and offered us a preferred lifestyle. So I produced another movie this time with the whole family as cast and crew but this time the location was France...

Sure enough, I attracted a business opportunity in Luxembourg – which meant that we could live in France, so again we immediately agreed and relocated back to Europe. We are still here – and rather than a new movie we are simply putting together the sequel – France 2 - the Monaco Years...

So what I have come to realise is that I don't like Goals – I like Movies, and once the Movie is clear in my mind my actions, behaviour and decisions are guided in such a way that the opportunities for the Movie to become a reality become open to me. My job is simply to recognise the opportunities and capitalise on them when they come along - my subconscious

The biggest challenge that people face in business and in life is that they either don't recognise the opportunity, or if they do they don't say YES, they think about it, procrastinate, find excuses, allow the fear to be stronger than the excitement- and end up doing nothing.

For example, working with me will change your life and change your business - I guarantee it. The only thing that holds people back is the debilitating activity of the logical mind which looks for evidence, certainty, guarantees and predictability. What great movie have you ever seen that had predictability or certainty in the script...?

Movies are products of creativity; use your creativity when making your decisions too...

The real beauty of this method, for me at least, is that when the phone rings and someone describes an opportunity – I can instantly either say yes or no, because if it is the right one, I will have already seen the movie in my mind and providing the two match, life is good.

Thursday, 5 July 2012

Goals Suck...

First, in order to understand achievement, we have to understand motivation...

There are four key drivers that motivate us;

- Achievement of a future Goal – *seeking pleasure* – towards motivation
- Relief from Pressure – *removing pain* – away from motivation
- Internal factors – *making us feel good to ourselves* – internal reference
- External factors – *making us look good to others* – external reference

This is why simply having a Goal doesn't work – it only satisfies one of the criteria – for a Goal to be engaging and motivational for us it needs to engage all of our drivers in the appropriate way.

First – let's clear up why Goals Suck...

Having a Goal would appear to be the panacea of achievement – there are books, videos, gurus and seminars that will tell you that Goals are the key to success and that without them you are useless. The Goals that they are talking about tend to be those that are future based – how many adverts have you seen that predict more money, better lifestyle and happier families. Network Marketers and Franchisors take note...

A Goal by itself is an excuse – it makes us feel good because we can carry with us the feint image of better times to come, but we don't ever have to achieve it because the "feel good" comes from imagining the possibility rather than actually achieving it.

If we feel good, or perceive the benefit of a Goal without actually having to achieve it, then we find excuses to do so...

In the 2006 movie Tristan and Isolde which is based on the 12th Century English legend known as Tristan and Iseult, the major issue regarding Goals is explained. In a scene where Tristan has conquered all before him and won the battle, he is sat on his throne looking forlorn.

Asked by one of his lieutenants why, after achieving everything that he set out to do, he is not full of joy, Isolde replies – "because he has lost the most precious thing he had – he has lost his dream..." or words to that effect...

Achieving a Goal means that we come to an end – the dream that we have becomes reality and as such the dream evaporates. Reality rarely lives up to the dream we have when creating it, so by definition the achievement of a Goal is a let-down. Paradoxically we cannot live without a dream or vision of our future and this is the very reason we are compelled not to actually achieve them – we simply want to keep the dream alive.

Friday, 27 July 2012

Entrepreneurs Only...

I am an Entrepreneur...

Not a serial entrepreneur – they simply jump from one bright shiny thing to another, using failure as an excuse for "learning opportunities"...

Serial Entrepreneurs think that failure is part of the journey – no its not – get it right first time, use knowledge skills and talent to make it right. When you have been on the receiving end of some of the "learning opportunities" that others have made, you will know how it feels.

Can things be improved..? –

Of course...

Are mistakes inevitable..? – Yes, but your clients should never know...

Is failure an option..? – Never...

My learning opportunities were when I worked in someone else's business and worked my way up, my learning opportunities were 14 years at night school, my learning opportunities were all the books I read, seminars I went to and experiences I had.

As serial entrepreneur is like serial husband or wife – no commitment to make something of true value actually deliver its full potential; when it gets too hard they simply move on.

No one wants one of those…

I am an Entrepreneur…

This is not what I do – *it is who I am…*

I do not have a career – *I have a life…*

I do not have a Job – *I make a contribution…*

There is no wage – *just reciprocated value…*

Hours – *as many as I choose and 1 more than necessary…*

Holidays – *life is a holiday, think of the alternative…*

Striking for better conditions – *I choose my own conditions…*

So when you meet a real entrepreneur who has put their heart and soul into what they do, when they have used their savings and begged and borrowed the rest and backed themselves 100% what should you say to them…?

Simple – "Well done…"

These people are the unsung heroes, they may not be all over Facebook, networking at champagne lunches, posting pictures from the Seychelles' – they will be building a business, figuring out how to pay the VAT, paying their staff before they pay themselves, riding around in a 15 year old car because all their cash is in their business and thinking how next quarter will be better than the last…

Be gentle with their dreams – what they build is all that they are, if you criticise their business you criticise them.

And when they make it, don't be jealous – don't think that success is easy and that they don't deserve it – they do…

If you want success in business – get to work, get to college, get to the library, get on with it, but most of all stick at it…

Serial Entrepreneurs are the pretenders to the Crown…

Are you an Entrepreneur…?

Monday, 24 September 2012

W.W.W....

One of the best known Acronyms in the World has a new meaning...

The Three Key areas, things we need to focus on when delivering Business Success...

1. Why - why do you do what you do...?

What is your true purpose - it's not the money, or at least it shouldn't be. Money is a consequence of everything that we do, but it is not Why we do it.

I have seen people in business simply chase the money without any thought or consideration for the contribution, difference or changes they could actually be making. In every case they end up both broke and alone or empty and unfulfilled.

2. What - what is in it for me...?

As a customer of yours, I will be asking myself the question - what is in it for me..?

What answer would I be able to give myself - what is the uniqueness of your product and service, what are the benefits to me...?

If you can't answer these questions, then nor can your Clients, if they can't taste the difference between you and a competitor then they will use price as a decision maker. If you are not positively differentiated in terms of Client experience and satisfaction - then you will be beaten down on price.

3. Wow - what is the WoW Factor...?

Do you go the extra mile or just do what the customer expected...?

How good would your service have to be that you never had to sell anything again - it was so good you had to ration it..?

Selling can be the art of getting people to part with their money on the basis of clever techniques rather than solid value. Do you have a WoW factor in your business - is everyone talking about you, do you have a waiting list..?

Monday, 24 September 2012

We are Not Broken...

The French Started it...

It was arguably a Frenchman called Emile Coue who began what we now know as the Personal Development movement - he would encourage people to simply affirm to themselves that "Every Day in Every Way I Am Getting Better and Better..."

Since this 19th Century pioneer, the movement has become awash with Coaches, Mentors, Gurus, Master Practitioners, Wizards and Pop Psychologists of every flavour.

The movement has some great and wise people doing amazing work - inspiring and teaching others how to lead happier more fulfilling lives, make more money and contribute positively to society and the world.

Around its rather tarnished and faded edges there are also those who, having achieved nothing of significance themselves, seek to simply regurgitate received knowledge in the vain hope that, whilst it didn't work for them - they will get paid enough money by others if they relay the ideas with enough conviction.

I went to a seminar earlier this year and was told that in order to become successful I had to overcome my limiting beliefs. I wasn't aware that I had such things, but I was assured that in fact I did, and unless I overcame them - I would be banished to a life of mediocrity and depression.

The clear message was that we were all broken and needed to be fixed - with a cocktail of visualisations, time line analysis, NLP and regression therapy. Much crying and sobbing ensued with "breakthroughs" being achieved in the dense embrace of a Kleenex tissue - I went to the bar for an early lunch...

But what if we weren't all broken - what if all these "Coaches" with zero on their personal and professional balance sheet, didn't have to bring the audience down to their level before they move forwards.

The skills that apparently qualify such gurus' include - working at the Council / Factory and being laid off, selling furniture, working as a waiter, having a breakdown / divorce / bankruptcy, being shouted at by the teacher and any number of other mind numbing experiments in banality.

Working with a Coach is the single best thing that any of us can do - so make sure you pick a good one.

Next time you are in touch with a Coach, Consultant, Master Wizard or Practitioner of any kind - check out their credentials - specifically;

1. **Relationships** - have they been able to have a long term stable relationship with anyone, ever...?

2. **Have they actually achieved anything of significance** - personally or professionally...?

3. **Are they using their own knowledge and ideas** - or simply those that have been found on Wikipedia or on the "Mind and Spirit" shelf at Waterstones.

4. **Do they assume you are broken and need fixing** - or amazing and simply need encouraging with some proven strategies...?

5. **Have they become a Coach** / Mentor / Wizard simply because they were laid off or became unemployable...?

6. **Are they** a person that you aspire to be like...?

If you cannot answer these questions to your satisfaction, move on and find someone to help you who actually cares enough about themselves and those around them to have achieved something amazing before they attempt to help others do the same.

Sunday, 28 October 2012

Twas the Night before Christmas...

Which Ghosts are guiding you...?

On Saturday Lynn was out partying with some of her friends - and us guys stayed in for a takeaway, ready for the call to go and collect the girls when they finally wanted to come home.

So we sat there drinking Coke and eating Prawn Crackers making conversation between us, although none of us actually knew each other that well. Now, guys will talk about cars, football, money and business - what struck me was not the subject of the conversation, but the context - *there appeared to be three main Ghosts in their Machines...*

1. **Ghost of Christmas Past** - the old days were better. Young people today don't have any respect and lack the knowledge to make a valuable contribution to the world. These guys were stuck in the past and were being guided by their dislike of the new.

2. **Ghost of Christmas Present** - their identity was purely based upon what they were doing right now. This was the power of the Ego - how everything that went well was due to their own personal efforts and anything that didn't - was the fault of someone else. They talked about how great they were, how much they knew and how everyone else was somehow less than them - they

were in fact the Alpha Males and their whole identity was defined by what they were at that instant. Apparently the brand and size of car is important here too...

3. **Ghost of Christmas Future** - the dreamers. We have lived in the USA and now we live in rural France - the journey has been and continues to be exciting...

    I really can't tell you the number of people (in the dozens...) who have told me that they would love to travel the world, live in Las Vegas or France and have a business that supported their lifestyle; rather than the other way round. What I can tell you is the number of people I have met that have actually done it - Three.

    The conversation occasionally moved to "what if scenarios" - however, for every positive there appeared to be three overriding negatives that meant the Dream would have to wait - for the Kids, the Business, the Money etc..

All these Ghosts are debilitating in their own way - the reality is of course that Ghosts only exist if we believe they do, or we choose to create them as a mechanism to cope with the FEAR of achieving our true potential - maybe it is time to look for alternative evidence to support a different belief structure.

Now we all have our Ghosts and Demons - but is there one that is dominating your life or business...?

Which Ghost is guiding you - is it time to move on..?

Friday, 23 November 2012

Contrary Marketing...

I have learned over time that I am contrary...

My tendency is to disagree with something - not because it is fundamentally flawed, but because I always prefer to adopt an alternative view...

This has been interesting both personally and professionally - and for Lynn, my wife since 1986, dinner discussions have always been "interesting"...

So when it came to Marketing, when I was told that I needed to "dominate" my sector, be front of mind in every prospect, be all over my market "like a rash" - I began to think..

What if what we did was so good that people hunted us down, we didn't need a web page, Facebook, LinkedIn or have to learn the 7 step sales process complete with navy blue suit, red tie and white shirt...?

What if we did the opposite of what everyone else does - everyone else by definition is only achieving average results after all...

In 1774, Frederick the Great - King of Prussia, wanted to introduce a second source of carbohydrates to the wheat (bread...) based diet of his subjects. The plan was to reduce dependence on a single crop, have alternatives should supply fail and introduce competition to the food market.

He sent out a Royal Order that farmers should grow Potatoes - the message was sent to everyone in Prussia, the Royal Marketing machine was in full swing. Not only was the marketing good, but it was compulsory too - so how could it fail...?

The response the Royal Court received from the peasant farmers was that potatoes were not good for eating; even the dogs wouldn't eat them. The refusal by the farmers to grow potatoes as a crop even resulted in executions of some of them.

Now, imagine a marketing consultant comes along...

The advice could have included suggestions that in order to correct this we need to target the market, come up with compelling offers and through a combined approach of Attention, Interest, Desire and Action the King could "dominate the market"...

Instead, the King applied a contrary approach - *I like him already...*

He withdrew potatoes from the market. He said that from now on, only the Royal Family could eat potatoes and they would only be allowed to be grown in the grounds of the Royal Palace - and they would be protected by armed soldiers from his personal guard.

Now, all good people know that if something is worth protecting with soldiers - it is also worth stealing - it must be valuable...

The guards were instructed to protect the crops of potatoes "badly" - and to turn a blind eye to anyone trespassing or stealing the crop. Pretty soon, illegal potato crops were sprouting up all over Prussia, and the potato became sought after as a staple alternative to wheat.

Frederick the Great thought the opposite of what intuition may have initially told him - or for that matter his equivalent of an MBA qualified Marketing Consultant... He kept his product a closely guarded secret, by using the principle of scarcity - and eventually achieved domination by doing the opposite...

What can we learn from this - simply to think in a contrary manner, go where the others don't; do the opposite of what the guru's say and you just might get the best results...?

Friday, 7 December 2012

String Theory

In parts of Asia where Elephants are used as beasts of burden, the trainers have developed a cunning plan that enables them to control the animals and keep them exactly where they want them.

It is so cunning in fact that it would be worthy of a Fox writing his final dissertation for his BSc in Cunningness at the University of Cunning – thanks Black Adder...

When Elephants are young and being trained, their keeper will tie one of their legs to a tree using thick rope. The Elephant objects and tries to pull away, but eventually learns that she cannot break the rope or pull the tree over.

Eventually, the Elephant gives in and becomes compliant – having learned that the tether she is restrained by cannot be broken. When she has learned this lesson, the keeper has the Elephant subdued and in one place by simply tying a piece of string to a sapling; whilst the Elephant has all the potential to snap the string or rip out the sapling by its roots, it doesn't - not because she can't but because she has been given the *belief* that she can't...

The Elephant has been conditioned, regardless of her physical strength or ability, to remain tethered, under the control of others through the use of a simple piece of string.

We know that she could easily break free, but she doesn't believe that she can so, she remains captive – even though freedom is just one easy pull away.

The question is – what strings are limiting you, what beliefs, fears or learned behaviours are synthetically restricting your freedom to be happy, successful and fulfilled..?

As with the Elephants, we sometimes learn to be constrained, and allow ourselves to fall into a pattern of behaviour that we believe is the only one available to us.

In reality of course, the strings that we allow to bind us are easily broken, it just requires us to make a simple decision, saying yes to an opportunity rather than "think about it..." choosing to move away from people and situations that don't serve us; or deciding that we simply deserve better…

So as it comes to the end of the year – consider what strings you would like to break for 2013. What decisions will you make, and what action will you take - *it is so much easier than you think...*

About Results Rules OK

Results Rules OK was created with a simple and clear 2020 vision;

To enable everyone to enjoy learning, achieving, doing and being more...

This is achieved through the delivery of World Class Business Coaching, Training, and Development Programs designed for business owners and entrepreneurs just like you...

We recognise that all businesses are different, as are the people that build, own and run them so we have a range of products and programs that will help, inspire and support you – whatever stage of development your business is at...

You can register for our newsletter, check out David's latest blog and even download documents and templates from our website at www.resultsrulesok.com

If you'd like to come along to an event – either to join one of our Webinars or participate in a Workshop or Seminar – visit our website www.resultsrulesok.com to find our full schedule of events.

David is offers a limited number of **FREE Business Strategy Sessions** for qualifying businesses, to arrange a meeting or discussion with David, simply got to www.resultsrulesok.com, scroll down and press the **"Big Red Button"** button...

Our USP is our people, our delivery, the results our Clients achieve and our philosophy of Fun in Life and in Business. We are a growing profitable business, and we believe in making contributions to charity and causes that are aligned with our values.

David's unique experience, background and passion for adding value to the business and personal lives of others have enabled him to become not only a top Business Coach, but an accomplished Speaker and Author. Having worked in 21 countries so far, his presentations and key note presentations are compelling, informative and fun and his books reflect his knowledge and personality…

David's first two books are available now…

If you have got this far then maybe we should talk…!

Contact Us;

Web – www.resultsrulesok.com

Email – info@resultsrulesok.com

Other Books by David Holland now available

Business Results Rules OK Volume I

Business Results Rules OK Volume II

Life Results Rules OK Volume I

Only Read at 4am

Would you like Fries with That?

Is Business Coaching Hornswoggle

Learning How to Fly

Unlucky for Some

The Case of the Ego in the Corner

The YOU Tree

Lights, Camera, Action

Contrary to Popular Belief

Every Day in Every Way, I'm Getting Better & Better

Success Matters

Success Rules OK

Scared of the Dark?

Leads United

Selling & Closing

The Franchise Connection

The Professional Tarot

Goals, Objectives and Precession

How to Surf the Tsunami…

Strength in Numbers….

Dutch Courage...

Negotiating Success

The 9 Rules

Drumming and the Art of Business Maintenance

The 5 P's Professionals need to know

Growing Pains

Fractional Thinking

Customers for Life

Presenting Excellence

Goals Suck

Excellence is a Real Pitch

So Good they Rationed it

Getting Picked

Changing Rooms

Smoke, Mirrors and Overnight Success

The End is Nigh

Symbiotic Results

Back to Front Leadership

Seeing is Not Believing

The Silence of the Pigs

Questions from your Favourite Teenager

The Time that People Forgot

The How 2 Series

The 4 Keys to Doubling your Business

Results RULES OK

The YOU Tree

Business Coaching
FOR Professionals
BY Professionals

Looking for someone inspirational, competent but also kind & honest? He's THE guy. A true leader that's always there to make you better.'

"David Holland MBA is FUN, he is extremely engaging and shares his wisdom generously with an intent to always be of service to others."

'David is always able to add just the right bit of humour to his professional endeavours'

'David is a superb coach with extensive business experience and knowledge - oh, and one of the funniest people I have ever met! '

www.resultsrulesok.com

www.ingramcontent.com/pod-product-compliance
Lightning Source LLC
Chambersburg PA
CBHW022128170526
45157CB00004B/1793